GOOD-BYE, ZOO

Written by Bob Egan
Illustrated by Margaret Sanfilippo

My brother took me to the zoo.

My mom told him he had to.

We zip past the zebra.

We zoom past the snake.

We zip past the yak.

We zoom past the lake.

I yell, "Good-bye, good-bye, zoo!
It was such fun to see you."